Crayola

COLORS of KINDNESS

A COLORING AND ACTIVITY BOOK

BuzzPop

COLORS OF KINDNESS

The Colors of Kindness crayon pack is all about encouraging you to get creative! There are over twenty-five shades, from Warm & Fuzzy to Life is Sweet. In this book, you'll color in images and complete activities using each shade in the Colors of Kindness pack. There are also stickers for added color fun! Check the back of the book for answers to the activities!

What's your favorite Colors of Kindness shade?
Color in this crayon with that color.

What can you do to show kindness today?
Use the name of your favorite color for inspiration!

Shell-ebrate yourself!
Color in this fun beach scene
and circle all the seashells you can find.

You are *berry* sweet!
Find your way to the strawberry patch so you can tend to your garden.

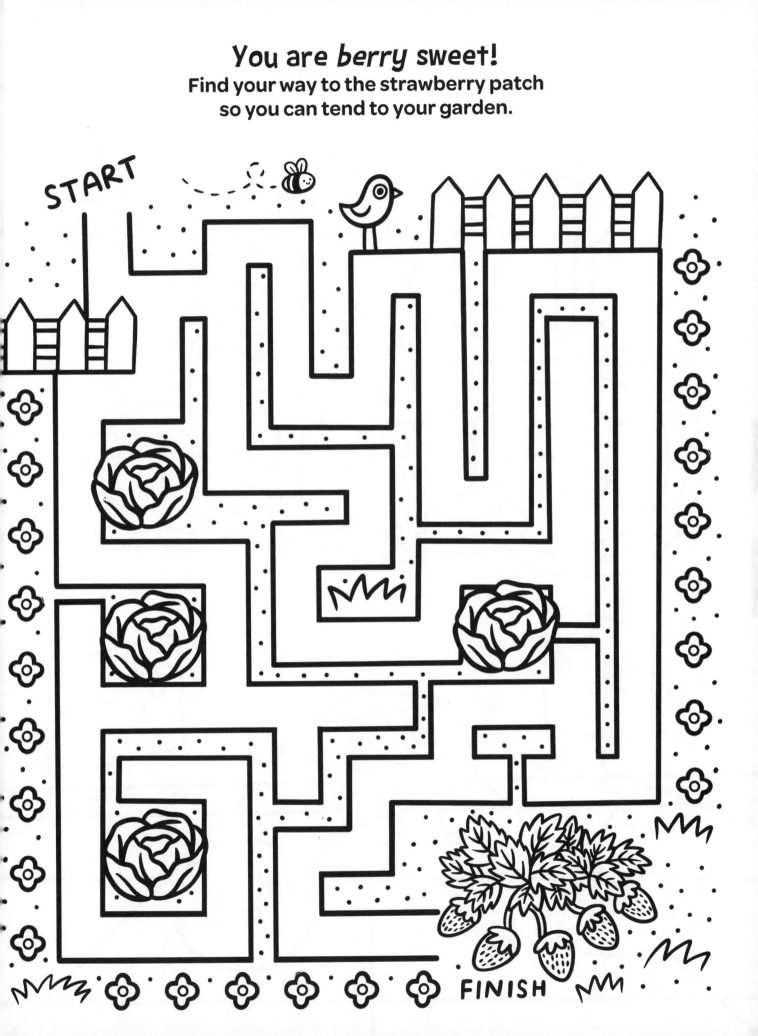

START

FINISH

Life is better with friends!
Draw a picture of you and your friends
on the perfect day. The *pasta*-bilities are endless!

Purr-fection!
Connect the dots to reveal what animal is looking cute and cuddly!

You are the best of the bunch!
What are your five favorite things about YOU?

1. _____

2. _____

3. _____

4. _____

5. _____

You shine brighter than the sun!
Draw a sun below and give it some shades.

Bear hug!

It's chilly outside! Connect the dots to help
warm up these bears! What are they wearing?

Party animals!
Throw a party to celebrate these animals by coloring them in with the brightest and most exciting Colors of Kindness!

Don't stop be-*leaf*-in'!

Can you guide these inchworms from one leaf to the next by pairing up the matching leaves? Draw a line to connect them!

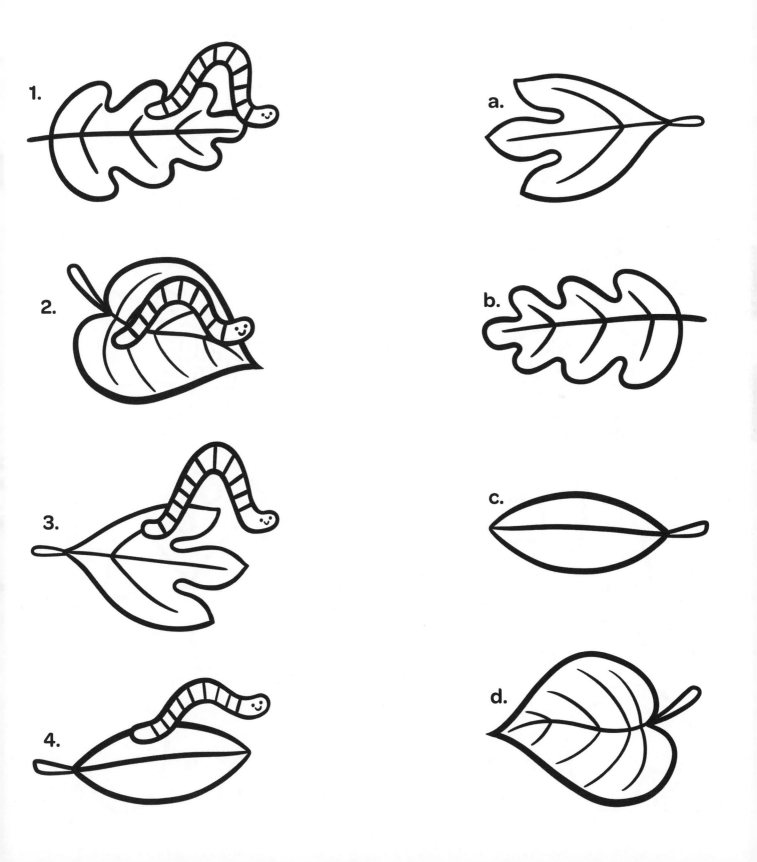

1.

2.

3.

4.

a.

b.

c.

d.

Who's the apple of your *pie*?
Bake them a pie to show how much you care.

TO:

LOVE:

Make a wish!
Color in the rainbow and then write a wish for yourself below.

I WISH:

You're *swell!*
Decorate these surfboards and make them uniquely you!

Ahoy, matey!
Help these sailors spot the treasure chest!

Bake time to rest.
Everyone should practice self-care.
Connect the dots to reveal this delicious treat!

Create your own Colors of Kindness!

You can create a one-of-a-kind color by mixing two existing Colors of Kindness! Color one crayon directly over another to make a brand-new shade. What's your unique color called?

Color in this scene and come up with as many new colors as you want!

This bird is *egg*-cellent!
Can you help this robin find her eggs?

START
A
B
C

FINISH

Reach for the sky!
How many clouds can you count?

Stand tall!

You are brave enough to handle anything life throws at you.
What are five brave things you can do this week?

1. _____

2. _____

3. _____

4. _____

5. _____

Out of this world!
Help the astronaut travel to a brand-new place!
Design a planet below.

Keep on soaring!
Draw yourself as a superhero.

I'm *rooting* for you!

Connect the dots to discover what object you can use to water these fruits and veggies.

Shoot for the moon!
Clear your head with a trip into space.
Can you help the rocket ship reach its destination?

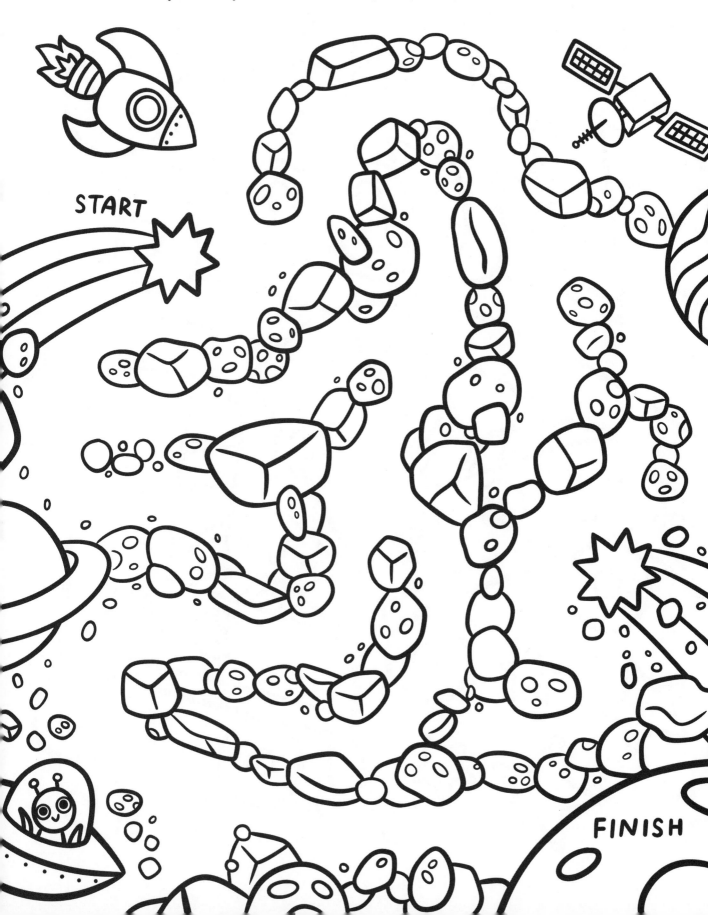

START

FINISH

We go together like . . .
Match these pairs to what they go best with.

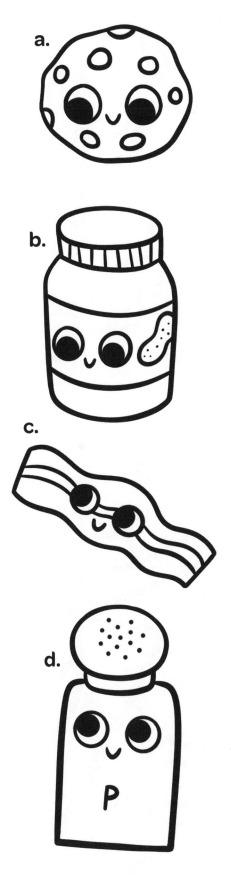

1.

2.

3.

4.

a.

b.

c.

d.

Keepin' it *cool.*
Follow the path that leads you to
your friend so you can share the ice cream!

Grow on!

Some flowers grow stronger when they are planted side by side. Draw two flowers in this empty flowerpot.

Color by number!
Each number in this scene corresponds to a different color.
Can you add the color back onto the page?

Key:

1: Hello Sunshine
2: Rise Above
3: A Slice of Nice
4: Go With the Flow
5: A Warm Hug
6: Lucky to Know You
7: Warm & Fuzzy
8: Sky's the Limit

You're as sweet as can be!
Circle all the sugary desserts!

What's the *scoop*?

Build the ultimate ice cream sundae to share with your favorite person.
What flavors would you include?

You *rock!*
Diamonds and jewels are shiny, but you dazzle me more!
What are five kind things you can do today?

1. _____

2. _____

3. _____

4. _____

5. _____

Flamin-*go* with the flow!
Connect the dots to reveal this loving shape.

Answer Key

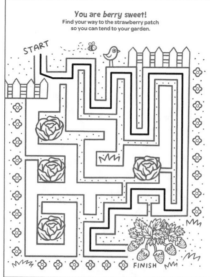

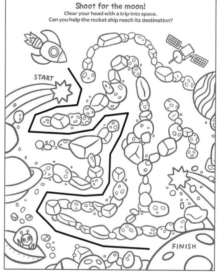

Matching:
Don't stop be-*leaf*-in'! Answers: 1. b.; 2. d.; 3. a.; 4. c.
We go together like . . . Answers: 1. d.; 2. c.; 3. a.; 4. b.

Counting:
Reach for the sky! Answer: 8 clouds

Connect-the-dots:
***Purr*-fection!** Answer: Cat
Bear hug! Answer: Scarf
***Bake* time to rest.** Answer: Gingerbread Person
I'm *rooting* for you! Answer: Watering Can
Flamin-*go* with the flow! Answer: Heart